The Dovekeeper &
the Death of a Child:
A Memoir

Till Heike

BookLeaf Publishing

India | USA | UK

The Dovekeeper & the Death of a Child: A
Memoir © 2024 Till Heike

All rights reserved.

No part of this publication may be
reproduced, stored in a retrieval system, or
transmitted, in any form or by any means,
electronic, mechanical, photocopying,
recording or otherwise, without the prior
written permission of the presenters.

Till Heike asserts the moral right to be
identified as the author of this work.

Presentation by *BookLeaf Publishing*

Web: www.bookleafpub.com

E-mail: info@bookleafpub.com

ISBN: 9789363312739

First edition 2024

For my daughters, Claudia and Michael, whose deaths and lives have changed me profoundly

I'm sure she is perfectly fine

I can barely move.
With every breath my diaphragm aches, and my
body stiffens with a rhythmic flow of pain.
The pain circulates through my body with my
blood.
Breathing in the sting, breathing out the burn, my
breath transitions from rough and hard to smooth
and rhythmic.
Slowly, slowly I bring my breathing to a point
where my mind can go past the pain—and
past that pain lies a list of unknowns about the
cause of this sudden and severe change in health.
It does not occur to me that something could be
wrong with my baby.
The pain radiates from my back and pierces my
shoulders, especially my left shoulder.
It does not affect my stomach at all. I know that
losing babies feels nothing like this.

So today, it isn't just my aversion to early mornings that keeps me in bed, in the early pale sunlight.
I lie there and focus.
I keep my mind on rhythmic breathing.
Keep breathing, slowly, so it doesn't sting too much.
Avoid flinching, because that hurts everywhere, but breathing hurts just half of me.
Breathe out the pain and wait, wait until I can hear life in the house.

2

The nurses in triage assign me a cot and wheel me into the 'holding dock' with my unspecified and vague description of pain in the vicinity of everywhere.

I slowly put my requisite green smock on, every movement planned in moments prior and accompanied by mental recitals of the word 'fuck'.

Try to remain as still and comfortable as I can. Regular breaths, in and out.

3

He orders some tests and in due course, all sorts of
blood and fluids are taken from me.
He certainly is not rude or inattentive, but seeing
me lying in the cot, smiling, he
assumes it isn't life-threatening.
Meanwhile I am still breathing in the sting and
breathing out the pain.

4

4

5

Time moves on and nothing is coming up on the tests.

Hormone levels are fine, bloods are fine. I realise they are running low on ideas when the doctor at one point politely suggests, 'When a petite woman becomes pregnant her body starts to expand and it can cause all sorts of sensations that you don't normally feel.

Your muscles and posture, combined with all those pregnancy hormones now coursing through your newly expanding body, will affect your ability to function as you did pre-pregnancy.'

They delicately, but not gracefully, get me on top of
the table.
All the pain returns.
I feel the nurses' hands come to aid me, and I make
it up inelegantly.

6

Her look is not worried, but it's the look of
someone who is thinking, and as the cogs tick over
in her brain, she wears it all over her face. This is
bad news.
She also mentions (a bit too casually) that I have
blood in my abdomen—a lot of blood.
She goes to call for another operator.

She puts her instrument down and leaves,
informing me she will be back with others.

8

They notice I am looking at them, not at the
screens, and ask me,
'Do you understand what we are telling you?'

8

9

I am swiftly admitted to a ward, and with a diagnosis at least mentally easing the bodily pain, I wait to hear from the doctor.

His happy reaction—yes you read that right, his happy reaction to seeing me is that he didn't 'need' to send me for that ultrasound, and that he was glad to have figured out what was going on.

My little bean, she's not in the right place. This one just happened to take out my fallopian tube with it. Collateral damage.
The physical pain has been as extraordinary singular as it was frightening.

I've died many times
yet again
I see,
the morning rise

a songbird spoke your name

Yes, you can say their name.
The sound is sweet to my ears.

When I hear it spoken
It's cinnamon toast and
rain-soaked leaves.
and broken hearts
and a million ways.

I yell,
you should be here.
warm in my arms
bedtime stories
left unread.

Counting toes
one, two, three, four, five,
all your little piggies
never came home.

Cinnamon toast
and tear-soaked cheeks

and the smell of baby born,
fresh and new.

I spoke your name when I held you,
I spoke your name when you had to go,
I spoke your name with whispers of sorrow,
And on the screams of grief

I say your name,
as mothers before me have
with love
with sorrow
with heartache
before unimagined

3

Moving forward means it will never now change
The experience must remain as it was
as it is
I cannot fight
I cannot change the outcome—
Not that I ever could

Sometimes I resent
when others tell me it's healthy
to move forward

It means I have to accept this for all it is
And it is simply so cruel
so unfair
so unjust

It still feels like the most unbearable pain
to not have you here

4

I will care for this little piece of Earth
the piece that holds tight to you
In honour of you
my sweetest and most powerful love
may these flowers always bloom
may we always have time to talk
In a way that feels like we are never alone.
I will sit and listen to all you have to tell me
and every time I enter the gates
and walk the worn out grass path
 that leads to your grave.
I will remind you
that my love never fades

Sleeping children
should be
warm in their beds
safe in their rooms
dreaming

7

on the shore's edge
holding onto thoughts
that you thought were common
Body ready to be enveloped with
warm salt water
Do we dare wash away the daydreams
of wolves daintily sat with tea
and a toad who sits with his long nose
upturned to the world
On the shore's edge I sit
holding thoughts that make me feel apart
but now they are old friends
coming back
to show me how to repair my home

8

With every rise and every fall
the waves are heavy enough
to hold me under
until there is no more
Last night I dreamt
I had a bird tangled in my hair
and your ghost beside me on the couch
cuddled up
smiling
A dead soul, and a head full of birds
It was perfect

12

A war-torn nation lay within me
I cannot even remember
what it means to be normal
Between waking and sleeping
are just fragile portraits of a moment

14

Little things lost
like hope
and trust
like naivety
and brevity
Don't tell me things happen for a reason
My daydreams are forever missing their pages

Prelude

Blown a kiss from Death herself

My whole body shudders and the violent
movement brings on further pain.
Crying makes my whole body jerk and causes me to
take deep, uneven breaths.
Each is excruciating.
After a minute, although my emotions are still not
under control, I try to calm my
breathing and keep my body still, because so far
that has been the only measure
that works at controlling the pain—even better
than any drug. It takes a few minutes
but eventually I take long, deep, even breaths.
my right fallopian tube has burst, I am now
bleeding into my abdominal cavity and
that is why I'm in so much pain.
Oh—and yes, the baby won't survive, if it's not
dead already.
I feel the duality and the contradiction.
I am empty, so empty.
Empty of a child, empty of the love, empty of its
future and us together; but I am

also full—physically, painfully full. Full of a river of
blood in my abdomen.
Full of the contents of a torn and ripped fallopian
tube that was no place for a baby to
grow. The emptiness hurts me emotionally, the
fullness hurts me physically. And I lie
covered in cold lubricant with strangers in a
hospital room that is only waiting for the
next patient, battered on both sides by something
that will never be.

The mirror is too big
Orange-yellow melancholia
letting wounds linger
tapered to dictate my grieving
my doing
and undoing
taper to nothing
a slow silent daydream of you

Little Songbird

The doctor checks growth.
All lovely.
As we pan down we catch a chubby little face
staring back, eyes squished shut,
cheeks all deliciously baby.
She opened her tiny mouth wide, perfect pillow lips
contorting, she gulped down the only
thing she can, and then gives an extended, adorable
yawn.
These three seconds pass like 20, such is the detail I
can see in her face as she
simply and so effortlessly expresses her annoyance
and disinterest at our
voyeurism.
In unison, three voices go 'Ah.'
The doctor winds back the frames on the monitor
to get a good screenshot of the
moment. The pictures I take home are the standard
ones of arms, legs and face, but
that delightful moment caught on camera, the
innocent yawn that would melt any

heart, looks odd in the static image, a poor
compromise of the original.
However, she was being adorable, and that is what
counts.
My next scan is at 33 weeks, I walk into the rest of
the day with a meandering joy.

22

The kids and I had browsed the bookshop earlier
that day, a wholesome and relaxing family outing.
The girls had disagreed, then agreed, then lost
interest, and became distracted and engrossed in
finding a book for themselves.
In that time, I managed to sneak off and look for
myself. A rare treat. I am planning
on upping my game in the final stretch of my
pregnancy, enjoying this third trimester
as I do, and I have found a suitable book to come
along with me.
The adage is, "Don't choose a book by its cover,"
but that is a large percentage of how I
choose them—I love a good cover, that's what
draws me in, then I read the blurb
and even out the difference.
This book is nice and long, but not too long, with a
pretty cover and an interesting blurb
Alice Hoffman's *The Dovekeeper*
That evening, I lay on my side, cradle my full belly,
open my book with a quiet joy, and read.

23

Besides the occasional chuckle from me, my only
interruption is my youngest daughter.
I can feel her moving around—large sweeping
movements, big extravagant stretches.
I call my husband's attention to it, and we smile at
our little acrobat in training.
The movements are so grand that the skin on my
belly aches as she pushes against it.
I make an involuntary 'whoosh,' Hubby looks over
to see her stretching my belly
straight out, we laugh, I adjust my seating.
I put my hands over my belly to comfort her and
pat. I stroke her feet as if
there is no skin between us. I pat her gently until
my gorgeous girl calms and goes to sleep.

Swinging on a cliff

It calls again at about 4 a.m.
This time hunger and a little unease keep me from
returning to bed.
I get up and make myself a cup of tea, sit in the
kitchen enjoying the quiet of the
early morning, and flick through the pile of school
notes that has gathered on the
countertop, seeing if there is anything that needs
immediate attention.
I move into the living room and finish my tea and
muesli while I watch the early morning/late night
European Soccer on television.
I notice that bub is not awake yet—usually she
hiccups or stretches in the morning.
Even when she sleeps she is prone to a roll around.
She usually bounces around for food or a drink.
Everyone is asleep
Peaceful
In hindsight, this is when I went into shock.

25

Her weight is still heavy in my womb and I take this
as a comforting sign that she is all right—such a big
baby.
I wish it was that simple.
Using my warm hands, I feel her feet through the
tight skin on top of my belly.
I tickle her toes and press the soles of her feet.
Whenever I do that, she always kicks back so I am
waiting for it, but she lets me push
them down.
My heart sinks.
She is not asleep.
Her weight feels heavy in my womb, such a big
baby.
My mind is on fire, the horses are long gone, the
barriers are in ruins. I can't control
them. My eyes won't blink, and won't move from
their blind gaze.
My surroundings remain unregistered; all I can see
is my panic as I stare blankly into
a black hole.

My eyes spill salt water and I don't blink it away, so
my hands wipe away silent tears
then settle to cradle my baby through the wall of
my abdomen.
Surely, she must still have my blood pumping
through her?
Even my fingertips pulse with the circulation of this
woefully inadequate mother's blood.

26

This is where everything I was before begins to die,
immediately and suddenly and
with no ceremony at all.

In black
I coil
a dance
of vague ambiance
or growing fear
horses rearing
at burgeoning gates
a tender cost
kept silent
don't even let out a whisper
of those words
don't let them
hear your fear
circling the gates
horses unbound

27

I, on the wing on a dove lay dying,
breathe,
shallow and still.

The doctor is gentle, soft-spoken, with a pleasant
bedside manner.
Obviously experienced.
His calm and sober demeanour during our brief
introduction, his slow and deliberate
style of walking and talking, speak volumes about
what he intends to do here today.
He's preparing himself as much as we are.
Does he know what happens next in my life? —
because I'm scared.
He perches on the edge of my bed and tells me the
gel will be cold, then puts the
scanner on my abdomen.
As clear as day, there is our daughter, bundled up
and snug.
But what is also immediately clear is that there is no
movement where a beating
heart should be.

My eyes dart around and settle on the read-out at
the bottom of the screen, the lines
where the pulses of steady rhythm should be
pounding out little grey mountains.
They show long, grey horizontal lines.
I am crying before he even says it, but he does, and
it came out like this:
'Your baby's dead.' It seems funny because he
makes it sound, in a professional way, as if
that is not quite what he was expecting, or maybe
that is just the way it hits my ears.
I can not control my reaction and sob
uncontrollably.
Worst fear realised.
I groan as I feel my heart ripping in two, burning
with pain.
It is a sound now etched into my psyche.
As I cry, my swollen belly moves up and down, and
I hold my hands over it to
cushion the jolting of my heavy uncontrollable
sobs.
The battle is lost.
We sit in this cold, sterile room and see only each
other, defeated.

28

Today is not in the script, how do I shield them
from sadness and death?
If the worst is happening to our unborn girl, there
is no way they can escape it. They
are looking forward to playing and growing up with
their new younger sister in the
same way I am longing to hold her in my arms.
Every avenue my mind wanders down carries a
burden I never thought I would have to
contemplate.

29

This feeling of having my power stripped bare,
my identity and self-worth obliterated, public
condemnation of my flaws as a human,
let alone as a mother. I
think about the emotional state of my husband. I
feel guilty for putting him through this.
I think about how I will have to handle this with
the kids, their emotions and grief.
They are so young, so full of innocence,
bubblegum and rainbows.
This will change their perception of the cycles of
life and death.
I don't want their bubbles to burst.

A stillness no scream can capture
Vainly folding hands between knees
a slow ruination
a fleeting glimpse of the winter sun
knots and knots in throats and words
be my nights unslept
an uncalm awake
of a restless mind

The Merrow's Song

In a place that is very far away but closer than a
dream, two shadows make their
way underneath the deep green water.
The two Merrows swam gently to the edge of the
lake, playful with childlike excitement;
What could be happening in such an isolated
corner of the lake?
Who would venture so far out?
The young mermaids heard the chattering of
strangers, lost heroes and life on the
land, curses, magic, lust, and love—could there be
such wonders in their future?
Many of the Merrow folk left at adolescence to
chance a human life on the lands,
nevertheless, these two had decided to stay in their
cool, ancestral waters.
They had found a devilish delight in singing to the
fishermen at night, driving some
half mad, and driving themselves into blustering
hysterics.
They found it amusing to listen to the myths of
their own heritage from the whispers

of the sailors as they trailed the boats through the
harbours in the lough and out to
safer waters.
The girls loved to play up their folklore, they could
often be found among the rocks of
the many islands sprawled throughout the lough
devilishly tapping on the bows of
vessels in their waters, keeping the fishermen awake
at night and only occasionally
messing with their catches.
The girls much preferred toying with the errand
and grander ships that would use
these waters as a thoroughfare.
The waters gave them freedom, the land was
plagued with mortal men, desirable to past
generations of Merrow, but the sisters
favoured the anonymity of the lake.
Maybe one day the pull of the land would
encompass them, however not yet.
With their tails sleek, and gossamer hair shining
under the cool green water, the
sisters shimmered their way slowly to the edge of
the lough.
They had come to this out-of-the-way grotto before
but it was not commonplace to have much activity

in this area, the county finished many leagues
south,
here only spirits and nomads grace these remote
shores.
These strangers were silent and deliberate in their
movements.
As the mermaid sisters came closer the carefree
feeling they displayed was
dissipating, the girls moved slowly even though they
were in no danger of being seen.
Humans were inattentive to the waters, but very
conscious of the land.
These strangers looked with intention at the terrain
around them.
Agitated and with low pitch they talked in muffled
bursts, and within moments and a candidly assured
shuffle, they had unloaded a heavy sack from the
cart.
The sack looked bleak and the sisters were cautious,
looking on with suspicion.
The burlier of the two men waded waist-deep into
the chilled midnight water, and
with a weighty heave, the sack was delivered to the
water.
As unceremonious as they arrived, the two men did
not look back as they abruptly left.

Leaving more tracks in the mud, then whispers in
the wind.
The dark side of humanity was not new to the
sisters, many a human body had found its way into
the lake, more often it was a sailor or fisherman,
who had wanted to live many times, die by the sea,
sometimes of his own agreement, sometimes not.
Even the surrounding counties would find occasion
to farewell the dead at the lake's shores.
With the Merrows always nearby to help the
deceased along the way, they
had much more contact with the human spirits
when they passed out of this material
realm to the next.
As they swan passively toward the hessian sack they
felt a breath, a feeling of
energy coming from the floating sack.
Dead humans have no energy left.
It's just a carcass. Maybe this wasn't just a carcass,
could it possibly not be dead?
Was it human at all?
The sisters had their doubts about that, the force
surrounding the sack was
palatable, something was not letting this earthly
energy pass, the sisters were
curious as they approached.

The sack floated like a damp brown island up to the
sisters and they circled the sack
curiously as it bobbed before them.
Murky brown hessian mirrored the disturbed
sediment on the rock shoreline.
The sisters, touching the hessian with gentle
fingertips, floated the sack towards the
nearest island, its occupant clearly in no hurry.
No human gave them this impression; this was
another realmer, someone who will
be missed. The sisters had to get this other to a safe
place so they could identify
them, no doubt there will be an absence that needs
to be recognised.

The girls wondered as they swam who this could
be; they whispered and giggled in
anticipation and worry, they were not involved in
the world of the land, whether
human, mortal or spectral. They were not affiliated
good or bad.

The sisters looked at each other over the top of the
sack, this looked like trouble, a delicious new piece
of trouble not of their making.

They smiled as the curiosity of getting involved in
someone else's mischief was too
enjoyable to hide.
The sisters approached and pulled the sack up to
the shore, their glistening tails
shimmering underneath the shallow waters so close
to the shore.

When Never Comes

The outcome for Claudia was already final
but the memory we carried forward of her
and her story within our family, was yet to be
written.
I resolved during the three to five-minute walk
across the hospital that if these were the
only memories I was to have of my daughter, I was
going to love her no matter what
personal hell I had to go through.
My lips were still quivering in reaction to the shock,
and my eyes were thumping as they were so swollen.
My brain was both like a burning fire ripping
through my thoughts, and a never-ending ocean of
calm.
The calm chaos of moments that you cannot move
around, only move through as best you can.

32

I am nervous in the morning when I realise it is
going to be a long day,
but by the afternoon I've become very calm.
The epidural has made me feel a bit more out of it
with every top-up.
The anaesthetists' arrival changes the demeanour in
the room for a short while,
shaking the sombre normality of the day, the
careful words, the downplayed eyes.
He is jovial—not overtly, not in a way that is
formed or rude, but he is a happy guy
going about his job.
We laugh a bit, we talk, we joke about how my
husband hates needles more than me, we laugh as
my husband turns pale at the sight of the imposing
epidural needle,
nearly fainting, his colour draining more as each
inch of the needle is pulled from the
packaging.
Oh, what a laugh, to laugh on a day like today, to
joke around, to be light-hearted in
words and actions.

As my husband lies on the long sterile bench a
metre away, I breathe deeply and
wait until the needling part is over, I bend my back
as instructed.
The deep orange-red of the Betadine goes on my
back in large sweeping swabs,
indicating a large working area.
I breathe deep.
I hope I don't become paralysed by the needle,
because although God knows I don't
think that will happen to me, that's the sort of
thinking that has brought me here—believing it
happens to others, not to me.
The needle finds it way in, my toes still move, and I
sit bent over with my swollen
dead belly cupped in my arms and cursed my
otherness.

33

How I just want to be part of the crowd right now,
the mass of people moving along
the path to the next comfortable destination, but
instead I'm here with her in my
arms, only skin between us, and him, the
anaesthetist, smiling while doing his job.
The banter dies down as he concentrates on the
task, and as he finishes, his jovial
mood shifts and he looks at me and says it's all in
properly.
He looks at me, making sure we are in a solid gaze,
and tells me how sorry he is that
I have to go through this.
I'm almost certain that once he leaves this room he
is going to the next suite to do
this all over again with another patient, with less
trauma.
I blink and thank him.
I silently wonder if this small interaction is what it's
going to be like from now on.
All fun and games until I'm somehow reminded
that I'm the mother of a dead baby.

Always a caveat, always a trauma lying beneath all the joyous moments I hope my life continues to bring.

34

All left so starkly unfinished
Have you ever cried like a lunatic?
felt a pain
a hurt
so deeply brewed
within you
that to release it is a begotten moan
leaves your body with such disregard for sanctity

Even though I wish to teleport myself three months
into the future, when I believe
everything will be settled back down, I have to give
my beautiful daughter a beautiful birth.
I have to see her safely into my arms and keep my
emotions in the positive spectrum as much as I can.

I can't be angry or bitter; that will only make her
birthday sorrowful and painful to
remember, so I keep myself in a state of calm
readiness in anticipation of meeting
her.
Of course, I am petrified, but I can deal with that
later—let's just get her here with no
more dramas.
The biggest drama has already come and gone
without a noise or a warning.

35

When the doctor finally breaks my waters at 7.30
p.m. it triggers heightened emotions in me.
I have been worried about what my daughter will
look like, her appearance, her skin
texture, her size; and the water breaking is a sign it
is all imminent.
The doctor has told me not to worry about these
things because at thirty-two weeks
'What will break your heart is that she will look
perfectly normal.'
These few unassuming and heartfelt words smack
me in the face and ring in my ears.
How very true.
Even the moment he says them, I can feel the
crushing truth in them.
I am shaking with the realisation that my perfect
daughter is still going to break my
already torn-apart heart.
The doctor takes a moment to busy himself writing
my medical notes. This is not
pleasant for him either.

He composes himself with a few deep breaths and I
try to do the same.
This is real and it is going to happen soon.
My deepest fear is just moments away.

36

Active labour begins at 9.45 that night, and at
10.33 Claudia Marie is born.
I have told the midwife already that if this was a
normal live birth I would have
wanted her put straight on my chest, as I had with
my other two.
I see no reason to change that now, and so with the
final push she is
scooped up and placed on my waiting chest.
She is warm, just like a newborn.
Perfect.
Absolutely perfect.
Perfect hands, perfect toes, nice chubby body.
Beautiful face, fine smattering of light
brown hair, fingernails, everything.

I cry as if my heart has been ripped apart anew.
I hold her and kiss her and try to soak in every detail
about her.
Through the tears, my eyes can't get enough of her.
I have to touch her and hold her and kiss her and
tell her how much I love her.

I stroke her beautiful face and wipe away a drop of
blood on her little button-nose

37

Every time you think heartbreak has reached its
peak, another moment comes along
to break it further into pieces.

Still Life

My heart imagines what joy we would have had just
to see her move her hand.
Her fingers are cupped on my chest and I long to
see them curl and splay.
To see her mouth pull open and let out a cry at the
abrupt motion of freedom from
her warm and happy home within the sobs of joy
and comforting arms of her parents.
Instead, our sobs are from sorrow and she never
moves to conform to my body, she
never nuzzles to find the milk my body drips for
her, she will never be comforted by
our kisses and words of love, to have our eyes meet
and know that she is home
I try to keep her warm, even though her body
becomes colder.

39

I'm off balance even with my feet flat on the tiles,
and I slowly shuffle out of the bathroom.
I see something that changes things for me,
something that will stay with me always
when I think of the day Claudia was born; it will
become one of my strongest memories.
I stand at the bathroom door, battered.
I can see the midwives have long ago taken
Claudia's measurements and are now
bustling around the suite.
However, one of them is sitting on a chair.
She has wrapped Claudia up and put her bonnet
on.
She is holding Claudia very close to her face, so
close they rub
noses.
I can see her lips moving.
She is talking to Claudia, a quiet conversation
between strangers, but you can see
the whispers hold so much love and sorrow.
It makes me so happy to see her holding Claudia
like this.

I am proud to be her mother, that beautiful baby is
mine and this wonderful lady
doesn't recoil at her but holds her as if she is any
other newborn.
She is rocking her gently, which is automatic when
holding a baby, even a quiet one.

Even, as it seems, a dead one.
Earlier I had done the same thing.
Instinct.
A mother's love is unstoppable.

She is
the gentleness
of the breeze
that follows stillness
The trace
of sweetness
that follows fingertips
Meandering atop
fresh spring growth
the weight of
a single breath
from lungs
collapsing

40

My body gives in some time later, I think when we
are still taking photos.
My blood pressure drops suddenly and sharply, and
I make it to a chair with no time
to spare. Laying my head on the bed trying to
regain a sense of consciousness.
The staff brings in a crib trolley and puts Claudia,
all washed, clothed and tucked up,
warm, though she herself is getting cooler.
They put me in a wheelchair and wheeled us both
through the maternity ward, the
nurses pushing me through the corridors and my
husband pushing his tiny
daughter's crib slowly so as to not jolt her.
I must have fallen asleep for ten to twenty minutes
because when I wake up I am in
the maternity ward with people coming and going
out of the room and lots of movement
all around. People are getting things ready in the
room, doctors and nurses are still
prodding me.

I am so tired, but the only thought I can hold in my head is that it is important to get Claudia next to me in bed.

41

I do not know how many nights together we will
have, but I know it is important to
have her next to me tonight.
With my depleted energy, I manage to get my
husband's attention, and ask him to
put her in bed with me.
He does, and I get to have one night of peaceful
dreams and shared warmth with my
newborn daughter lying next to me; face to face, my
arms around her all night, I
breathe her in all night, filling myself with her scent.
I stay in bed and silently cry, to think she was just a
flicker away from being
alive, so peacefully asleep she appears.

42

All my heart whispers goodnight,
As stars sail you softly
to adventures untold
Blue skies and lullabies
and filaments of gold